MEDICATION SAVINGS UNLOCKED

NAVIGATING INSURANCE AND CUTTING COSTS

EXPERT STRATEGIES TO UNDERSTAND INSURANCE AND REDUCE YOUR MEDICATION EXPENSES

Dr. Rhowela A. Friel, PharmD

DISCLAIMER

This book is intended for informational purposes only. The author and publisher make no representtations or warranties regarding the completeness, accuracy, applicability, or suitability of the content contained herein.

The information provided is not a substitute for professional medical advice, diagnosis, or treatment. Always consult a licensed healthcare provider regarding any health-related concerns or before starting, changing, or discontinuing any treatment or medication.

The author and publisher expressly disclaim responsibility for any loss, injury, or damage—personal, medical, legal, financial, or otherwise—that may result from the use or misuse of the information presented in this book.

Mentions of medications, products, or brand names are for illustrative purposes only and do not imply endorsement. All trademarks and brand names are the property of their respective owners and are acknowledged accordingly. Their inclusion does not constitute an infringement of intellectual property rights.

By reading this book, you agree that neither the author nor the publisher shall be held liable for any direct, indirect, incidental, special, consequential, or punitive damages arising from its use. This disclaimer applies globally, regardless of your country of residence or where the book is purchased.

The content reflects the author's professional knowledge and experience as of the publication date and may evolve with advances in medical research. The material is provided "as is" without any warranties. If you do not accept these terms, you should discontinue use of this book.

Copyright © 2024 by Rhowela Albana Friel

All rights reserved.

No portion of this book may be reproduced in any form without written permission from the publisher or author except as permitted by U.S. copyright law.

DEDICATION

To my husband—thank you for always believing in me, especially when I struggled to believe in myself. Your quiet support and steady love helped bring this book to life.

To our girls—you are my reason, my joy, and the heart behind every page.

And to you—if you're holding this book, know that it was written for you. For the questions you're carrying, the care you're giving, and the strength you don't always see. I'm so glad you're here.

Rhowela A. Friel, PharmD

WELCOME!

Before you get started, I just wanted to say thank you—for picking up this book, for caring enough to look for answers, and for being the kind of person who shows up when it matters.

I also wanted to let you know I've built a space online to keep the support going: rhowelaafriel.com.

It's where I share what I've learned (and keep learning) as a pharmacist, a mom, and someone who knows how overwhelming care can feel sometimes. You'll find free resources, gentle tools, and updates on what's coming next. No noise, no pressure—just what might actually help.

And if this book made things a little clearer or calmer for you? Leaving a quick review helps others find their way here too.

I'm so grateful you're here.

Rhowela A. Friel, PharmD

TABLE OF CONTENTS

DISCLAIMER i

DEDICATION iii

WELCOME! v

INTRODUCTION 9

Chapter 1: Understanding Health Insurance 11

    1.1 Health Insurance Basics 11

    1.2 Understanding Primary vs. Secondary Insurance 13

Chapter 2: Navigating Insurance for Medications 17

    2.1: Prior Authorizations Explained 17

    2.2: Insurance Formularies and Cost Savings 19

Chapter 3: Strategies for Reducing Medication Costs 25

    3.1: Generic Vs. Brand-Name Drugs 25

    3.2: Finding the Best Pharmacy Deals 27

    3.3: Utilizing Patient Assistance Programs (PAPs) 29

    3.4: Exploring Therapeutic Alternatives 31

Chapter 4: Maximizing Savings and Program Discounts 33

    4.1 Discounts and Coupons 33

    4.2 Discussing Alternative Medications 35

Chapter 5: Understanding Your Rights and Resources 39

    5.1 Appeals Process and Patient Rights 39

    5.2 Medication Refunds and Rights 42

    5.3 Legal Rights and Advocacy 44

Chapter 6: Navigating Government Health Programs 49
  6.1: Types of Government Programs................................... 49
  6.2: State Pharmaceutical Assistance Programs (SPAPs). 57
  6.3: The 340B Drug Pricing Program 59
  6.4: Case Studies and Real-Life Examples........................... 62
  6.5: Practical Tools 66

Chapter 7: Practical Tools and Resources............................... 69
  7.1: Checklist and Templates 69
  7.2: Free Vaccine Resources 71
  7.3 Interactive Tools 73

Chapter 8: Financial Assistance for Medications................... 77
  8.1 Introduction to Financial Assistance............................ 77
  8.2 Non-Profit Organizations 78
  8.3: Crowdfunding for Medical Expenses.......................... 80
  8.4: Government Grants and Programs 82

Further Reading And Resources 85

CONCLUSION... 91
  Key Takeaways 91
  What You Can Keep Doing.. 93

ACKNOWLEDGMENTS... 95

ABOUT THE AUTHOR 97

MORE SUPPORT 99

INDEX.. 101

INTRODUCTION

Hi, if you're here, there's a good chance you've run into the same frustrating wall that so many of us have: medication that costs too much, insurance that's confusing (at best), and no clear answers when you need them most.

I've seen it firsthand—as a pharmacist, and as someone who's helped thousands of people try to make sense of this system. And here's the truth: it doesn't need to be this hard.

That's why I wrote this book.

It's not here to overwhelm you or give you a million new things to figure out. It's here to simplify what matters—so you can spend less time on the phone with insurance companies and more time actually taking care of yourself or your loved ones.

What This Book Covers

This book walks you through the most important parts of saving on medication, step by step:

- How insurance works and what terms like deductibles, formularies, and prior authorizations really mean

- What to do when a medication isn't covered or costs too much

- Smart ways to find discounts, coupons, or patient assistance programs

- Tools and checklists you can actually use at your next pharmacy visit or provider appointment
- Government programs and financial help that might be available to you—even if no one's ever mentioned them before

I've broken it all down into clear, manageable chapters—so you can either read from start to finish, or just jump to the section that fits what you're dealing with right now. No pressure. No fluff.

Use this book however it helps you most. And remember—you're not alone in this.

CHAPTER 1: UNDERSTANDING HEALTH INSURANCE

Hello! In this first chapter, we'll talk about how health insurance works. I'll explain the basics of insurance policies and help you understand the difference between primary and secondary insurance. It's important to know how these policies affect your healthcare so you can make the best choices for yourself and your family. Let's dive into how you can manage multiple insurance policies without getting lost in the jargon!

1.1 HEALTH INSURANCE BASICS

Understanding health insurance is key to managing both your health and your wallet. Health insurance helps cover the high costs of healthcare services and medications. Here are some important terms and concepts to get started.

Key Insurance Terms Explained

- **Deductibles**: This is the amount you must pay for healthcare services before your insurance starts to help. For example, if your deductible is $1,000, you have to pay the first $1,000 of your healthcare costs each year.

- **Co-pays**: These are set fees you pay for specific medical services or prescription pick-ups. For example, a co-pay could be $25 for a doctor's visit or $15 for a medication refill.

- **Co-insurance**: After you've reached your deductible, co-insurance is the percentage of the cost of a service that you pay. For example, if you have a 20% co-insurance rate and the service costs $200, you will pay $40 while insurance covers the remaining $160.

Formularies

A formulary is a list of medications covered by your insurance plan, which often includes both generic and brand-name drugs. Medications on this list are typically less expensive, so it's good to choose these options when possible.

Hack: Always keep a current copy of your formulary handy. It can change; what was covered last year might not be this year. You can often choose your insurance based on the coverage of your current medications. Usually, your insurance plan has a helpline to help you pick the best plan.

Practical Examples
Imagine your prescription drug costs $200, and you've already reached your annual deductible. If your co-insurance rate is 20%, you will pay $40 out of pocket for that medication, while your insurance covers the rest, $160. But if your plan has a co-pay of $15 for medications, you will only pay that amount, no matter the total cost.

1.2 UNDERSTANDING PRIMARY VS. SECONDARY INSURANCE

Handling your coverage when you have multiple health insurance plans can feel tricky. But don't worry—I'm here to make it easier. Understanding primary and secondary insurance can help you save time and get the most benefits.

Primary vs. Secondary Insurance Explained
- **Primary Insurance**: This insurance plan pays first when you have a healthcare expense. It covers part of the costs based on your plan's benefits before any other insurance is considered. If you are employed and have insurance through your job, this is usually your primary insurance.

- **Secondary Insurance**: This kicks in after your primary insurer has paid its part, covering any extra fees or co-pays that the primary did not cover. Think of it as a safety net that helps lower your out-of-pocket costs.

Coordination of Benefits (COB)

This is the process by which your insurers talk to each other to decide who pays first (primary) and who pays later (secondary). The goal is to avoid duplicate payments. If you are insured by your spouse's and your employer's policies, one will be primary and the other secondary, based on specific rules set by the insurers.

Hack: If your insurer denies a claim because it thinks another insurer should cover it, contact both insurers to coordinate benefits. Your insurers need to know if they are the primary or secondary. Typically, insurance from your job is the primary insurance, and your spouse's coverage is secondary. If you have two jobs, the primary is the job where you work the most hours. This step is important to avoid out-of-pocket expenses.

Hacks for Managing Multiple Policies

1. **Document Everything:** Keep a record of all your insurance policies, including contact information, policy numbers, and what each policy covers.

2. **Regular Reviews:** Regularly review your insurance policies, especially during open enrollment periods, to make sure they still meet your needs and that you are maximizing your benefits.

3. **Clear Communication:** Clearly communicate with your healthcare providers about your primary and secondary insurance to ensure that claims are filed correctly.

Step-by-Step Guides

How to Choose a Health Insurance Plan

1. **Assess Your Needs:** Consider your health needs, including any ongoing treatments or medications.

2. **Compare Plans**: Look at different plans and compare their coverage, costs, and network restrictions.

3. **Check the Formulary:** Ensure your medications are covered.

4. **Calculate Costs:** Consider premiums, deductibles, co-pays, and co-insurance.

5. **Seek Help:** Use resources like healthcare.gov or contact an insurance advisor.

Filing Claims
1. **Gather Documents:** Collect all necessary documents, including receipts and medical records.

2. **Fill Out the Form:** Complete the insurance claim form with accurate information.

3. **Submit the Claim:** Send the form and documents to your insurance company.

4. **Follow-up:** Check the status of your claim regularly until it is processed.

Wrapping it all up...
Thanks for joining me in exploring the basics of health insurance! By now, you should have a clearer understanding of how your insurance works and the differences between primary and secondary insurance. Remember, the better you understand your insurance policy, the more effectively you can use it to cover your healthcare needs. Keep this chapter in mind as you navigate your insurance options and make informed decisions.

CHAPTER 2: NAVIGATING INSURANCE FOR MEDICATIONS

In this chapter, we'll explore how to manage your medication costs through insurance. I'll explain what prior authorization means and how you can handle it smoothly. We'll also look at insurance formularies to understand what your insurance covers and what it doesn't. By the end of this chapter, you'll feel more in control of your medication expenses and confident in managing your insurance benefits.

2.1: PRIOR AUTHORIZATIONS EXPLAINED

When you're ready to start a new medication but encounter a roadblock called prior authorization, it might feel like a major inconvenience.
Understanding why it's necessary can simplify the process and help guide you through your next steps.

The Reason Behind It

Prior authorizations are a process that insurance companies use to make sure the prescribed medication is both necessary for your treatment and is a cost-effective option.

Steps You Can Take

Once the pharmacy informs you that your medication needs prior authorization, call your healthcare provider and let them know. This will speed up the process. Your provider needs to give your insurance more details about your medication so it can be covered. Following up with both your provider and your insurance company can help move things along faster.

Pro Tip: Write down how your condition affects your daily life. This will help your doctor explain to your insurance company why you need this specific medication.

Hack: Remember that prior authorizations are all about insurance coverage. If you can't wait for approval or you're willing to pay on your own, tell your pharmacist you want to proceed without insurance. Ask about savings through discount cards or manufacturer coupons. You can also ask your pharmacist to suggest an alternative medication covered by your insurance and get a new prescription from your doctor.

Step-by-Step Guide: How to Request a Prior Authorization

1. **Contact Your Doctor:** Inform your healthcare provider that a prior authorization is needed.

2. **Provide Information:** Make sure your doctor has all the necessary details about your medication and condition.

3. **Submit the Request:** Your doctor submits the prior authorization request to your insurance company.

4. **Follow-up:** Check with your doctor and insurance company to ensure the request is processed.

2.2: INSURANCE FORMULARIES AND COST SAVINGS

Looking into insurance formularies might not sound exciting, but it's worth it if you want to save money on medications. An insurance formulary is a list of medications your insurance prefers and covers. These medications are chosen based on how well they work, how safe they are, and their cost. Formularies are often divided into tiers. The higher the tier, the more you pay out-of-pocket.

Medication Tiers

- **Tier 1: Generic Medications**:
  These are the cheapest options. They are generic versions of brand-name drugs and have the same active ingredients, strength, and dosage forms as the brand-name products but cost much less.

- **Tier 2: Preferred Brand-Name Medications**:
  These are brand-name medications that the insurance pays for at a higher cost than generics but less than non-preferred drugs. They are chosen for their affordability and effectiveness.

- **Tier 3: Non-Preferred Brand-Name Medications**:
  This tier covers brand-name medications that are not recommended because there are cheaper generic or preferred brand-name alternatives. These drugs require higher copays or coinsurance. This tier might include newer, more expensive medications without generics.

- **Tier 4: Specialty Medications**:
  These are costly prescription medications often used to treat complex, chronic diseases like cancer, multiple sclerosis, and rheumatoid arthritis. They may need special handling, administration, or monitoring. Specialty medications are often the most expensive for patients out-of-pocket.

Hack: Find out which tier your drug is in. If it's higher than Tier 1, ask your pharmacist or doctor if a generic or lower-tier alternative could work for you.

How to Use Formularies for Savings

1. **Review Your Plan's Formulary**: Get the most recent version of your insurance's formulary. It's usually available on the insurer's website or by contacting customer service.

2. **Discuss Alternatives with Your Healthcare Provider**: If you're prescribed a high-tier medication (more expensive), ask your doctor about possible lower-tier alternatives. There could be a generic or another brand-name prescription that is just as effective but cheaper.

3. **Check for Updates**: Formularies are reviewed and can change every year. A medication that was covered at a lower cost one year may move to a higher tier the next year. Stay updated to avoid unexpected costs.

4. **Appeal Decisions**: If you're taking a medication that isn't on the formulary or is in a higher-cost tier, you and your doctor can appeal to your insurance company. Providing documents explaining why a specific medication is important for your health may lead to coverage exceptions.

5. **Ask Your Pharmacist for Help**: Your pharmacist is a great source of information about your insurance formulary. They can suggest alternatives and help you navigate your plan.

Pro Tips and Hacks for Expediting the Process

1. **Keep Documentation**: Keep thorough records of all communications with your healthcare provider and insurance company. This includes dates, times, and names of the people you spoke with.

2. **Use Technology**: Many insurance companies and healthcare providers have online portals or apps where you can check the status of your prior authorizations and formularies, submit documents, and communicate with support staff.

3. **Be Persistent**: Follow up regularly with your healthcare provider and insurance company. Persistence can often speed up the approval process and ensure your needs are met quickly.

Wrapping it all up...

We've covered a lot about managing your medication through insurance, including prior authorizations and understanding formularies. With these tools, you can confidently handle your medication coverage and know exactly what your insurance will and won't pay for. Use this knowledge to avoid surprises and manage your healthcare budget more effectively.

Rhowela A. Friel, PharmD

CHAPTER 3: STRATEGIES FOR REDUCING MEDICATION COSTS

Let's talk about saving money on your medications! This chapter focuses on choosing between generic and brand-name drugs and finding the best deals at pharmacies. I'll share some great tips on how to shop around and choose cost-effective medications without compromising quality. Get ready to cut your medication costs significantly with some smart shopping strategies!

3.1: GENERIC VS. BRAND-NAME DRUGS

When you visit the pharmacy, you may be given two options for the same medication: the brand name or its generic. Let's clarify some common questions, help you understand the differences, and explain why generics can be a smart choice.

What Makes Them Similar

Generic medications are comparable to brand-name drugs because they have the same active ingredients, safety profiles, potency, dosage forms, route of administration, quality, and intended use. It's like comparing two recipes for the same meal made by different chefs; the final result is essentially the same.

The Price Gap Explained

Why are generics often much less expensive? Well, generic drug manufacturers don't bear the initial costs of developing and marketing a new drug, which brand-name companies do. Once the brand-name drug's patent expires, other companies can create a generic version of the drug. This competition often results in cheaper prices, with generics costing roughly 80-85% less on average.

Hack: Always ask if there is a generic version of your medication. Choosing generics whenever possible will drastically lower your medication expenses while maintaining quality and effectiveness. By choosing generics, you're making an informed decision about your health and managing your healthcare budget more effectively.

3.2: FINDING THE BEST PHARMACY DEALS

Let's look at how you can get the best pricing for your medications. The cost of medications varies between different pharmacies, and a bit of savvy shopping might lead to big savings.

Price Comparison Tools

Price comparison tools, such as GoodRx and SingleCare, provide real-time price comparisons between pharmacies. By entering the medication name, you can see where it is being offered at the lowest cash price (without insurance) in your area, potentially saving you a significant amount on each prescription.

Leveraging Pharmacy Programs

Larger pharmacy chains such as CVS and Walgreens have programs that allow them to search through their database of discount programs to find the best offer for each medication without insurance, including finding manufacturer coupons.

Considering Independent Pharmacies

While big chains are everywhere, it's important to consider your local independent pharmacy. Independents often offer reasonable rates and personalized care that you may not find elsewhere. They are also more likely to offer specialty services, like custom medication packaging, that can make it easier for you to keep track of your medications.

The Mail-Order Option
Mail-order pharmacies can be beneficial for managing chronic conditions and ensuring consistent medication delivery. They not only provide lower costs for larger orders, but they also deliver directly to your door, saving you time and hassle.

Hack 1:
Paying Without Insurance - Smart Shopping
When paying out of pocket for generic medications, consider exploring prices at big retailers like Walmart or wholesalers like Costco. These outlets often offer lower prices for generics, making them a cost-effective choice. They also provide services for pet prescriptions, which might be cheaper than purchasing directly from your vet. Doing a little homework to compare prices could lead to significant savings.

Hack 2:
Utilizing Insurance at Preferred Pharmacies
If you're using insurance to pay for your medications, it pays to know which pharmacies your plan prefers. Preferred pharmacy status can mean lower co-pays and overall costs. Check with your insurance company or review your benefits paperwork to identify your preferred pharmacies. Taking advantage of preferred status can optimize your savings, especially when filling brand-name or specialty medications.

3.3: UTILIZING PATIENT ASSISTANCE PROGRAMS (PAPS)

Patient Assistance Programs (PAPs) can be a lifeline for those struggling with medication costs. Pharmaceutical companies usually pay for these programs, which give free or cheap medications to people who apply.

Steps to Apply for PAPs
1. **Research Available Programs**: Start by researching available PAPs for your medications. Websites like NeedyMeds and RxAssist provide comprehensive lists of programs.

2. **Check Eligibility Criteria**: Each program has its own eligibility criteria, often based on income level and lack of insurance coverage.

3. **Gather Required Documentation**: Be prepared to provide documentation such as proof of income, prescription details, and possibly a letter from your healthcare provider.

4. **Submit Your Application**: Follow the application process, which may involve submitting forms online or via mail. To avoid delays, make

sure all the necessary information is included.

Case Studies of Successful Applications

Case Study 1: Jane's Story

- **Background**: Jane, a 45-year-old single mother, was prescribed an expensive medication for her chronic condition. With no insurance, she struggled to afford her treatment.

- **Solution**: Jane's healthcare provider recommended a PAP. She applied, providing the necessary documentation, and was approved. The program covered her medication costs, saving her $500 a month.

Case Study 2: Mark's Journey

- **Background**: Mark, a 60-year-old retiree, faced high costs for his heart medication despite having Medicare. His limited income made it challenging to manage these expenses.

- **Solution**: Mark applied for a PAP through the medication manufacturer. With his income documentation and a letter from his cardiologist, he was approved. The program reduced his out-of-pocket costs by 75%.

3.4: EXPLORING THERAPEUTIC ALTERNATIVES

Therapeutic alternatives can be another effective way to reduce medication costs. These alternatives might include different medications that achieve the same therapeutic effect but are less expensive.

Explanation of Therapeutic Alternatives and Their Benefits

Therapeutic alternatives are medications that, while not chemically identical, offer similar therapeutic benefits. For example, different medications within the same drug class may be used to treat high blood pressure.

How to Discuss Alternatives with Healthcare Providers

1. **Be Informed**: Research potential alternatives before your appointment.

2. **Ask Questions**: Discuss the efficacy, side effects, and costs of alternatives with your provider.

3. **Consider Your Health History**: Ensure any alternative is safe and effective for your specific health needs.

Examples of Common Therapeutic Alternatives for High-Cost Medications

- **Example 1**: Substituting a high-cost brand-name cholesterol medication with a lower-cost generic alternative within the same drug class.

- **Example 2**: Using an over-the-counter antihistamine instead of a prescribed allergy medication.

Wrapping it all up...

I hope this chapter has given you some valuable strategies to reduce your medication costs. Whether it's choosing generics, finding the best pharmacy deals, utilizing patient assistance programs, or exploring therapeutic alternatives, these tips can lead to significant savings. Keep these strategies in mind each time you fill a prescription, and remember, every little bit adds up to substantial savings over time.

CHAPTER 4: MAXIMIZING SAVINGS AND PROGRAM DISCOUNTS

Did you know there are many programs and discounts that can help you save on medication costs? In this chapter, we'll talk about how to find and use discounts, coupons, and assistance programs. We'll also discuss how to talk to your doctor about cheaper medication options. These strategies are here to help you save money while still getting the treatments you need.

4.1 DISCOUNTS AND COUPONS

Understanding how to cut the cost of your medications can save you a lot of money. Let's look at the tools you can use to make medications more affordable:

Discount Cards and Coupons

- **Discount Programs**: Programs like GoodRx and SingleCare offer big discounts on medications. By using their websites or apps, you can compare prices at different pharmacies and find the best deal. These programs can turn a $100 medication into something more manageable, like $40.

- **Manufacturer Coupons**: These coupons come directly from pharmaceutical companies and are especially helpful for newer or brand-name medications. They can sometimes provide free fills or significantly reduce co-pays. You can find these coupons on the manufacturer's website or through your pharmacy.

Hack: Take advantage of the help offered by larger coupon programs like GoodRx. They have a customer service department that can help you with price issues and offer extra support. Don't hesitate to use these resources to maximize your savings.

Step-by-Step Guide to Using Discount Programs

1. **Visit the Website or Download the App**: Go to GoodRx or SingleCare websites or download their apps.

2. **Search for Your Medication**: Enter the name of your medication to see the available discounts.

3. **Compare Prices**: Look at the prices at different pharmacies near you.

4. **Print or Show the Coupon**: Print the coupon or show it on your phone at the pharmacy.

4.2 DISCUSSING ALTERNATIVE MEDICATIONS

If you're facing a high co-pay or your medication isn't covered, don't hesitate to ask your pharmacist for alternative options. There might be a similar medication that's just as effective but at a lower cost.

How to Approach Pharmacists and Doctors

- **Be Honest**: Clearly explain your financial situation and ask for their help in finding a more affordable alternative.

- **Ask About Generics**: Always ask if there's a generic version of your medication.

- **Request a Review**: Ask your doctor to review your current medications and suggest lower-cost alternatives that are just as effective.

Hack: While your pharmacist can start the conversation about switching medications, contacting your healthcare provider directly can speed up approval. Your doctor may respond faster if you contact them directly, speeding up the switch to a more affordable medication option.

Tips for Switching to More Affordable Alternatives

- **Therapeutic Substitution**: If a generic isn't available, ask about therapeutic alternatives—different medications that provide the same benefit.

- **Dosage Adjustments**: Sometimes, adjusting the dosage or frequency of your medication can reduce costs without compromising effecttiveness. Before you make any changes, you should always talk to your healthcare provider.

Case Study:

John's Story: John was prescribed a brand-name cholesterol-lowering drug that cost him $150 per month. After discussing his financial concerns with his doctor, he switched to a generic version that cost only $15 per month. This switch saved him $1,620 annually.

Additional Tips for Maximizing Savings

1. **Use Multiple Discount Programs**: Sometimes, different programs offer different savings. Check several programs to find the best deal.

2. **Ask About Pill Splitting**: Some medications can be safely split, allowing you to buy a higher dose and use half, saving money. Always check with your doctor first.

3. **Look for Assistance Programs**: Some non-profit organizations offer assistance for specific conditions. Research programs related to your medication.

Interactive Checklist for Tracking Savings

- ☐ Check for generic versions of your medication.
- ☐ Compare prices using discount programs.
- ☐ Ask your doctor about therapeutic alternatives.
- ☐ Look for manufacturer coupons.
- ☐ Research patient assistance programs.

Wrapping it all up…

By now, you should feel more equipped to take advantage of various programs and discounts that can help lower your medication costs. Don't hesitate to discuss cheaper medication alternatives with your doctor and make full use of the discounts available to you. Remember, asking for help and seeking out discounts is a smart way to manage your healthcare expenses.

CHAPTER 5: UNDERSTANDING YOUR RIGHTS AND RESOURCES

It's important to know your rights as a patient. This chapter will guide you through the appeals process if your insurance denies coverage for medication and how to argue your case. We'll also look at your rights regarding medication refunds and exchanges. Knowing these rights can help you stand up for your health needs and ensure you're treated fairly.

5.1: APPEALS PROCESS AND PATIENT RIGHTS

When you get an insurance denial for a medication or treatment, remember that it's not necessarily the final word. You have options and the right to contest their decision. Let's break down the appeals process so you can confidently advocate for your healthcare needs.

Initial Steps in the Appeal Process

1. **Understand the Denial**: Carefully read the denial letter from your insurance company. It will explain why the coverage was rejected and outline the steps to appeal.

2. **Gather Documentation**: Work with your health-care provider to gather supporting documents, such as medical records, scientific papers, and personalized letters, to explain why the specific medication or treatment is necessary.

3. **Submit Your Appeal**: Follow your insurer's rules for appealing, which often involves organizing your gathered evidence and submitting it within a specified timeframe.

4. **Seek Support**: Don't hesitate to ask for help from your doctor, a patient advocate, or a loved one. They can guide you through the appeals process and help present the strongest possible case.

Hack: If your initial appeal is denied, don't give up. Many insurance plans offer multiple levels of appeal. Persistence can often lead to a successful outcome.

Building Your Case
1. **Personalized Letters**: Your doctor can write a detailed letter explaining why the specific medication is necessary for your treatment.

2. **Scientific Evidence**: Include research studies or clinical guidelines that support the use of the medication for your condition.

3. **Patient Impact Statement**: Describe how the medication improves your quality of life and the potential consequences of not receiving it.

Step-by-Step Guide to Filing an Appeal
1. **Understand the Denial**: Carefully read the denial letter from your insurance company.

2. **Gather Documentation**: Collect all necessary documents, including medical records and letters from your doctor.

3. **Submit Your Appeal**: Follow the instructions in the denial letter to submit your appeal.

4. **Follow-up**: Check with your insurance company regularly until your appeal is resolved.

5.2: MEDICATION REFUNDS AND RIGHTS

Let's talk about something we hope you never have to deal with, but it's good to be aware of if you do: medication refunds. You may end up paying more for your medications than necessary, whether due to a pharmacy error or a delay in filing your insurance claim. But don't panic; you have options.

Getting a Refund from the Pharmacy

1. **Identify the Error**: Check your pharmacy receipts and insurance statements for any discrepancies.

2. **Act Quickly**: Most pharmacies have a limited window (often within 14 days) to issue a refund for overcharges. Contact them as soon as you notice the error.

3. **Provide Documentation**: Be prepared to provide receipts, insurance statements, and any other relevant documentation to support your claim.

Dealing Directly with Your Insurance

1. **Missed Refund Window**: If you missed the pharmacy's refund window, contact your insurance company directly to explain the situation and request a refund for any overpayments.

2. **File a Claim**: Follow your insurance company's procedures for filing a claim for reimbursement. This may involve submitting receipts and a written explanation of the overpayment.

Practical Advice: Always save your pharmacy receipts and keep track of your insurance claims. Identifying and correcting discrepancies early on is key to avoiding overpaying for your prescriptions.

Hack: Many insurance companies have online portals where you can track your claims and payments. Regularly review this information to catch any errors quickly.

Step-by-Step Guide to Getting a Refund

1. **Identify the Error**: Check your receipts and insurance statements.

2. **Contact the Pharmacy**: Reach out to the pharmacy to report the error and request a refund.

3. **Provide Documentation**: Submit any necessary documents to support your claim.

4. **Follow-up**: If needed, contact your insurance company for further assistance.

Case Studies

Case Study 1: Sarah's Refund Success

- **Background**: Sarah noticed a $50 overcharge on her pharmacy bill. She quickly checked her insurance statement and confirmed the error.

- **Solution**: Sarah contacted the pharmacy within a week, provided her receipts and insurance statement, and received a refund within a few days.

Case Study 2: Mike's Insurance Claim

- **Background**: Mike missed the pharmacy's refund window for an overpayment.

- **Solution**: Mike contacted his insurance company, explained the situation, and filed a claim with supporting documents. His claim was approved, and he received a refund for the overpayment.

5.3: LEGAL RIGHTS AND ADVOCACY

Understanding your legal rights can empower you to take control of your healthcare. Let's explore some key rights and resources available to you.

Overview of Patients' Legal Rights

- **Right to Information**

    You have the right to receive accurate and easily understandable information about your health plan, healthcare professionals, and healthcare facilities.

- **Right to Choose Providers**

    You have the right to choose healthcare providers who give you high-quality healthcare when you need it.

- **Right to Privacy**

    Your healthcare information must be protected, and you have the right to privacy.

How to Seek Legal Help and Advocacy

- **Patient Advocates**

    Many hospitals and healthcare facilities have patient advocates who can help you understand your rights and assist with disputes.

- **Legal Aid Organizations**

    Non-profit organizations provide free or low-cost legal assistance to those who qualify. They can help with insurance appeals, denials, and other healthcare-related legal issues.

Organizations that Provide Support and Resources

- **Patient Advocate Foundation**
  Offers case management services to help patients with insurance appeals and denials.

- **National Health Law Program**
  Provides legal support and advocacy for low-income individuals facing healthcare issues.

- **HealthCare.gov**
  Offers information on patient rights and resources for finding legal assistance.

Additional Tips

1. **Stay Informed**: Regularly review your health insurance policy and stay updated on any changes that might affect your coverage.

2. **Keep Records**: Maintain thorough records of all your interactions with healthcare providers, pharmacies, and insurance companies.

3. **Ask Questions**: If you're unsure about your rights or the appeals process, ask for clarification from your insurance company, healthcare provider, or a patient advocate.

Checklist for Tracking Appeals and Refunds
- ☐ Understand the Denial
- ☐ Gather Documentation
- ☐ Submit Your Appeal
- ☐ Follow Up Regularly
- ☐ Identify Errors in Pharmacy Bills
- ☐ Contact the Pharmacy for Refunds
- ☐ Provide Necessary Documentation
- ☐ File Insurance Claims if Needed

Wrapping it all up…

By understanding your rights and knowing how to navigate the appeals process, you can effectively advocate for your healthcare needs. Remember, you are not alone—there are resources and support systems available to help you.

Rhowela A. Friel, PharmD

CHAPTER 6: NAVIGATING GOVERNMENT HEALTH PROGRAMS

In this chapter, we'll navigate the landscape of government health programs like Medicare, Medicaid, CHIP, and the VA. I'll explain what these programs cover, how you can qualify, and how to access state pharmaceutical assistance programs and the 340B drug pricing program. This information will help you use these programs to lower your drug costs and improve your healthcare experience.

6.1: TYPES OF GOVERNMENT PROGRAMS

Medicare

Eligibility and Coverage
Medicare is a health insurance program for people over 65 and younger people with certain diseases or disabilities, like end-stage renal disease (ESRD).

Part D of Medicare helps with medication costs, which can be a huge relief.

- **Medicare Part A (Hospital Insurance)**
  Covers hospital stays, care in a skilled nursing facility, hospice care, and some home health care. Most people don't pay a premium for Part A if they or their spouse paid Medicare taxes while working.

- **Medicare Part B (Medical Insurance)**
  Covers certain doctor services, outpatient care, medical supplies, and preventive services. There is a monthly premium for Part B, which is deducted from your Social Security benefits if you're receiving them.

- **Medicare Part C (Medicare Advantage Plans)**
  An alternative to Original Medicare, offered by private companies approved by Medicare. These plans must cover all services that Original Medicare covers except hospice care. Most plans offer extra coverage, such as vision, hearing, dental, and health programs, and include Medicare prescription drug coverage (Part D).

- **Medicare Part D (Prescription Drug Coverage)**
  Adds prescription drug coverage to Original Medicare and some other types of Medicare

plans. There is a monthly premium for Part D, and the cost varies by plan.

Hack: Use the Medicare Plan Finder tool on the official Medicare.gov website. This tool can help you compare Part D plans to find one that covers your medications at the lowest cost. If you're on a tight budget, look into the Extra Help program, which helps with Medicare prescription medication costs.

Example: Sarah, a 67-year-old retiree, used the Medicare Plan Finder tool and found a Part D plan that significantly reduced her medication costs. She also qualified for the Extra Help program, further lowering her expenses.

Medicare.gov is a great resource for detailed information on eligibility, benefits, and enrollment. You can also call 1-800-MEDICARE for personalized help. Understanding your healthcare coverage can greatly affect your health and finances.

Medicaid

Eligibility and Coverage

Medicaid helps low-income individuals and families, children, pregnant women, the elderly, and people with disabilities. The eligibility criteria vary by state since both federal and state governments fund the program, but they generally consider income, family size, and disability status.

- **Eligibility**: Covers low-income adults, children, pregnant women, elderly adults, and people with disabilities. Each state may have different income thresholds and requirements.

- **Coverage**: Includes doctor visits, hospital stays, long-term medical care, custodial care, and more. Each state maintains a list of covered medications.

Hack 1:

Check your state's formulary to see which medications are covered. If your prescribed medication isn't on the list, ask your doctor about prescribing a covered alternative or requesting a Medicaid formulary exception.

Hack 2:

Look into Medicaid's Managed Care plans if your state offers them. These plans may include extra benefits and medication coverage options. Many states also have support programs to help you navigate Medicaid and maximize your coverage.

Example: Tom, a 45-year-old with a disability, found that his state's Medicaid Managed Care plan covered additional therapies and medications that regular Medicaid didn't, significantly improving his quality of life.

Medicaid's website for your state and Healthcare.gov are good starting points for eligibility criteria, benefits, and enrollment processes. Applying for Medicaid can significantly lower healthcare costs, including prescription medications. Always keep up to date on your state's specific Medicaid options since they can change and offer new benefits.

Dual Eligibles—Medicare Part D and Medicaid Combined

Eligibility and Coverage

If you qualify for both Medicare and Medicaid, you have a unique advantage in covering your healthcare and prescription drug needs.

- **Eligibility**: Dual eligibility means you qualify for both Medicare and Medicaid. This typically applies to low-income seniors and younger individuals with disabilities.

- **Coverage**: Medicare Part D is your primary plan for prescription drugs. Medicaid acts as a secondary payer, covering extra costs that Medicare doesn't, such as certain medications or co-pays.

If you're eligible for both Medicare and Medicaid, they work together to keep you covered. It's like having a healthcare tag team in your corner, ensuring you get the care and medications you need without high costs. Additionally, being dual eligible means you automatically get Extra Help under Medicare Part D, which lowers prescription costs, premiums, and co-pays.

Example: Mary, a 70-year-old dual eligible, saved hundreds of dollars each month on her medication costs by using both Medicare Part D and Medicaid. The Extra Help program further reduced her out-of-pocket expenses.

Children's Health Insurance Program (CHIP)

Eligibility and Coverage

The Children's Health Insurance Program (CHIP) helps children in families whose incomes are too high for Medicaid but too low to afford private insurance.

- **Eligibility**: CHIP eligibility varies by state but generally covers children in families with incomes too high for Medicaid but too low to afford private insurance. Some states also cover pregnant women.

- **Coverage**: Includes routine checkups, immunizations, doctor visits, prescription drugs, dental and vision care, and emergency services.

Hack 1: CHIP also has a formulary. If the prescribed medication isn't covered, ask your pediatrician or family doctor to switch to a covered alternative or help you apply for a formulary exception.

Hack 2: CHIP programs differ by state, so learn about the advantages and enrollment dates in your state. Some states treat CHIP as an extension of their Medicaid program, while others have separate or merged CHIP programs.

Example: Laura's children received comprehensive healthcare through CHIP, including dental and vision care, which relieved a significant financial burden from her family.

The official CHIP website in your state, usually accessible through the state health department's website, and InsureKidsNow.gov are good resources for learning about eligibility requirements, benefits, and application procedures. Using CHIP coverage for your children's prescriptions ensures they have access to necessary medications and helps you manage your family's healthcare costs.

VA Health Care

Eligibility and Coverage

The VA healthcare system provides millions of veterans with a wide range of medical, surgical, and rehabilitation services.

- **Eligibility**: Depends on various factors, including discharge status from military service, length of service, service-connected disabilities, and income level.

- **Coverage**: Offers primary care, specialized care, mental health services, and home health care. Veterans may also qualify for the VA Medication Copayment Program, which helps reduce the cost of prescription medications.

Hack 1: One lesser-known benefit of the VA healthcare system is its mail-order pharmacy. It's very convenient, especially for veterans who live far from VA medical facilities or have mobility issues.

Hack 2: Depending on your priority group, you may be eligible for reduced or no-cost co-pays. Verify your eligibility and enroll in the proper priority group to reduce out-of-pocket costs. If you are having financial difficulties, the VA provides assistance programs to help with prescription co-pays.

Hack 3: If your VA provider recommends OTC medications, ask them to write you a prescription. This allows you to get them from the VA pharmacy or through mail-order at no cost.

Example: Robert, a Vietnam veteran, used the VA mail-order pharmacy to get his medications delivered to his home at no cost, saving him time and money.

The VA's official website (va.gov) is a helpful resource for learning more about the VA healthcare system, eligibility, and benefits. Local VA hospitals and clinics are also available to help with enrollment and answer any concerns you may have.

6.2: STATE PHARMACEUTICAL ASSISTANCE PROGRAMS (SPAPS)

Eligibility and Benefits

State Pharmaceutical Assistance Programs (SPAPs) aim to provide financial support to eligible individuals for prescription medications. They typically focus on seniors, those with disabilities, and low-income residents.

- **Eligibility**: Eligibility criteria for SPAPs can vary greatly by state. In general, they consider age, residency, income level, and current Medicare Part D or Medicaid coverage.

- **Coverage**: SPAPs provide a variety of benefits, including covering co-pays, deductibles, and even medications not covered by Medicare Part D.

Hack: If you have Medicare Part D, SPAPs can help you cover costs that Part D does not cover. It's a good idea to find out how the two can work together to your advantage. SPAPs may provide additional support where Medicaid falls short, particularly in states where Medicaid prescription coverage is limited.

Example: Alice, a 72-year-old senior, found that her state's SPAP covered the cost of her diabetes medications, which were not fully covered by Medicare Part D.

Your state's health department is a wealth of information about SPAP eligibility and application processes. Additionally, Medicare.gov and Medicaid.gov offer information on how SPAPs work with federal programs.

Important Considerations
- **Timing is Key**: Keep an eye on SPAP enrollment times to avoid missing out on potential benefits. These times may not always coincide with Medicare Part D enrollment periods.

- **Documentation**: To make the application process go more smoothly, prepare any relevant documentation ahead of time, such as income verification, Medicare or Medicaid information, and medical prescriptions.

State pharmaceutical assistance programs (SPAPs) provide an important support system for managing prescription costs, especially for people currently on Medicare Part D or Medicaid. While the regulations and benefits of SPAPs differ by state, understanding these programs can result in significant savings and peace of mind.

6.3: THE 340B DRUG PRICING PROGRAM

Imagine stepping into a pharmacy and finding that your prescription costs are much lower than elsewhere. That's the power of the 340B Drug Pricing Program, a little-known gem in the healthcare system.

Overview of the 340B Program

The 340B Drug Pricing Program is a federal program that helps people in underserved communities or those struggling with medication costs to get their prescriptions at lower prices. It's managed by The Health Resources and Services Administration (HRSA), part of the U.S. Department of Health and Human Services (HHS). The program provides benefits regardless of insurance status and may offer other resources like health screenings, free vaccinations, patient education, and counseling.

Eligibility and Coverage
- **Eligibility**: Primarily for people receiving outpatient care from certain hospitals and clinics, especially those in rural areas serving many low-income, uninsured, and undocumented patients. These healthcare providers can buy medications at much lower prices and pass the savings on to you.

- **Coverage**: The 340B program covers a wide range of outpatient medications. It's particularly useful for managing chronic conditions like diabetes or HIV/AIDS, where medication costs can add up quickly.

Hack: Anyone is eligible, regardless of income, as long as they are seen at a 340B participating facility, are seen by a 340B healthcare provider in that facility, and fill their prescription at a 340B contracted pharmacy, often attached to or near the 340B participating facility.

Finding the Right Place for Your Prescriptions
The first step is to identify healthcare providers, hospitals, or clinics that participate in the 340B program. You can find these entities using the HRSA website's "Find a Health Center" link. Make an appointment and discuss your medication needs and any additional support services you may require during your visit. Your healthcare provider can

guide you through the process and help you effectively use the benefits of the 340B program.

For those wanting to learn more about the program, the Health Resources and Services Administration (HRSA), which supervises the 340B program, has a wealth of information on its website. Additionally, 340B Health, an organization for program providers, offers resources to help you navigate the system.

Hack: To get the best discounts, fill your prescriptions at a pharmacy participating in your healthcare provider's 340B program. You can often get medications at very low prices, including no co-pays. Some 340B participating Health Care Centers might also offer free health screenings or educational resources, so don't forget to ask about what's available.

The 340B Program allows eligible healthcare organizations and covered entities to buy medications at much lower costs. It's designed to stretch limited federal resources to provide more comprehensive services and reach more patients. While patients don't sign up directly for this program, asking your healthcare provider if they participate can result in lower costs on medications and other healthcare benefits.

6.4: CASE STUDIES AND REAL-LIFE EXAMPLES

To better understand how these programs work, let's look at some real-life examples and case studies that show how people have successfully used these resources to reduce their healthcare costs.

Case Study 1: Navigating Insurance for Cost Savings

Background: John, a 65-year-old retiree, was struggling with high medication costs despite having Medicare coverage. His monthly prescription costs were eating into his fixed income, causing financial stress.

Challenges:

- High out-of-pocket costs for brand-name medications
- Difficulty understanding Medicare Part D coverage
- Limited knowledge of available discount programs and assistance

Strategies Implemented:

- **Switching to Generics**: John consulted his doctor about switching from brand-name medications to generics. His doctor identified equivalent generics that were just as effective but significantly cheaper.

- **Reviewing Medicare Part D Plan**: During the Annual Enrollment Period, John used the Medicare Plan Finder tool to compare different Part D plans. He found a plan with better coverage for his medications and lower out-of-pocket costs.

- **Using Discount Programs**: John signed up for GoodRx and SingleCare, using these discount cards to lower his medication costs further.

Outcome: By switching to generics, finding a better Part D plan, and using discount programs, John reduced his monthly prescription costs from $300 to $80. This substantial saving allowed him to allocate funds to other essential expenses.

Case Study 2: Leveraging Patient Assistance Programs

Background: Maria, a single mother of two, was prescribed a costly medication for a chronic condition. Without insurance coverage for this medication, she faced a monthly bill of over $500, which was unaffordable on her income.

Challenges:
- High cost of necessary medication
- Ineligibility for certain insurance plans
- Lack of awareness of assistance programs

Strategies Implemented:

- **Applying for Patient Assistance Programs (PAPs)**: Maria's pharmacist informed her about the pharmaceutical company's PAP for her medication. She applied and was approved for free medication.

- **Using Manufacturer Coupons**: For another medication, Maria used a manufacturer coupon to reduce the cost significantly.

- **Exploring Community Resources**: Maria contacted local health organizations that provided additional support and resources.

Outcome: Through the PAP, Maria received her expensive medication at no cost, saving over $500 a month. Using manufacturer coupons and community resources further reduced her overall healthcare expenses, making her financial situation more manageable.

Case Study 3: Effective Communication with Healthcare Providers

Background: David, a 45-year-old professional, was diagnosed with hypertension and prescribed multiple medications. Concerned about the long-term costs, he sought ways to manage his expenses without compromising his health.

Challenges:
- High co-pays for multiple medications
- Concern about the affordability of long-term treatment
- Limited understanding of medication options

Strategies Implemented:
- **Discussing Medication Costs with Doctor:** David had an open conversation with his doctor about his financial concerns. His doctor recommended a single, more affordable medication that effectively managed his condition.

- **Requesting Samples and Coupons:** David asked his doctor for samples and manufacturer coupons, which provided immediate cost relief.

- **Exploring Mail-Order Pharmacies:** David switched to a mail-order pharmacy for a 90-day supply of his medication, reducing the cost per dose.

Outcome: David's proactive approach and open communication with his doctor led to a more affordable medication regimen. By using samples, coupons, and mail-order services, he reduced his monthly medication expenses by 50%.

6.5: PRACTICAL TOOLS

To help with these processes, here are some practical tools you can use:

Checklist for Finding the Best Medication Prices

- ☐ **Review Medication List**: Make a list of all your medications, including dosage and frequency.

- ☐ **Check for Generics**: Ask your healthcare provider if there are generic versions of your medications.

- ☐ **Compare Prices**: Use tools like GoodRx and SingleCare to compare prices at different pharmacies.

- ☐ **Explore Mail-Order Options**: Check if a mail-order pharmacy can provide your medications at a lower cost.

- ☐ **Apply for Assistance Programs**: Look into PAPs and manufacturer coupons for your medications.

- ☐ **Discuss with Your Doctor**: Have an open conversation with your healthcare provider about your financial concerns and ask for more affordable alternatives.

Appeal Process Guide

1. **Understand the Denial**: Review the denial letter to understand why coverage was denied.

2. **Gather Documents**: Collect supporting documents, including a letter from your doctor, medical records, and relevant research.

3. **Write the Appeal Letter**: Include your personal information, details of the denial, and your argument for coverage.

4. **Submit the Appeal**: Follow your insurer's appeal process, including any deadlines.

5. **Follow-Up**: Keep track of your appeal status and follow up as needed.

Wrapping it all up...

We've explored various government health programs available to help manage your medication and healthcare costs, along with practical examples and tools to aid in the process. With this knowledge, you can determine which programs you might be eligible for and understand how to apply for and benefit from them. Remember, these programs are here to help you, so take advantage of them to improve your health and reduce your expenses.

CHAPTER 7: PRACTICAL TOOLS AND RESOURCES

In this chapter, you'll find tools and resources that will help you use the strategies we talked about earlier. These practical aids will help you get the most out of your healthcare plan.

7.1: CHECKLIST AND TEMPLATES

Prior Authorization Checklist

This checklist guides you through the steps of getting prior authorization for a medication. It helps ensure you have all the needed documents and information.

Checklist:
- ☐ Contact your healthcare provider to request prior authorization.
- ☐ Gather supporting documents (like medical records and physician's notes).
- ☐ Submit the prior authorization request to your insurance company.

- ☐ Follow up with your healthcare provider and insurance company.
- ☐ Confirm approval or appeal if denied.

Appeals Letter Template

If your insurance claim is denied, use this template to write an effective appeals letter. Customize it with your details and supporting documents.

[Your Name]
[Your Address]
[City, State, ZIP Code]
[Email Address]
[Phone Number]

[Date]
[Insurance Company Name]
[Address]
[City, State, ZIP Code]

Re: Appeal for Denial of Coverage for [Medication/Service]

Dear [Insurance Company],

I am writing to appeal the denial of coverage for [medication/service] prescribed by my healthcare provider, Dr. [Provider's Name]. This medication is important for managing my [condition] and improving my quality of life.

Enclosed are supporting documents from my healthcare provider, including medical records and a letter explaining the necessity of this treatment. I kindly request a review and reconsideration of my case.

Thank you for your attention to this matter.

Sincerely,
[Your Name]

7.2: FREE VACCINE RESOURCES

Getting the vaccines you need can be hard if you don't have health insurance. But there are many ways to get these important shots for free or at a low cost. Knowing where to find these resources can help protect your health and stop the spread of diseases.

Vaccines for Children (VFC) Program

The VFC program gives free vaccines to kids under 18 who are on Medicaid, don't have insurance, or whose insurance doesn't cover vaccines. Clinics and doctors in this program provide the shots kids need. To find out more, visit the CDC's VFC page at www.cdc.gov.

Health Departments in Your Town and State

Local and state health departments often have programs to give free or low-cost vaccines to people without insurance. They offer shots for flu, hepatitis, HPV, and more. Check your local or state health department's website for information. You can find your local health department through the National Association of County and City Health Officials at www.naccho.org.

Federally Qualified Health Centers (FQHCs)

FQHCs, also known as community health centers, provide many health services at low or no cost based on what you can afford. They offer vaccines and other important health services, especially in areas with few medical facilities. Find a center near you using the locator tool at findahealthcenter.hrsa.gov.

Pharmacy Programs
Some pharmacies offer free vaccination programs, especially during health campaigns. Big pharmacy chains sometimes work with health groups to give free flu shots and other vaccines like shingles or pneumonia. Visit or call your local pharmacy or check their websites for more information.

Charitable Organizations and Clinics
Non-profits like the American Red Cross and local clinics often hold free vaccine events for uninsured and low-income people. Look for information in community centers, local newspapers, and online. Check the websites or call these organizations for upcoming events.

School-based Health Centers
Schools often have health centers that give free vaccines, especially in low-income areas. These centers make it easy for kids to get shots like flu and HPV. Check your school district's website or contact your child's school for more information.

Community Outreach and Health Fairs
Community health fairs and outreach programs often offer free vaccines. These events are usually run by hospitals, health departments, or community

groups. Look for information in community centers, churches, and local websites.

7.3 INTERACTIVE TOOLS

Online Calculators for Estimating Medication Costs

Using online calculators can help you manage your medication expenses. These tools let you enter details about your medications and insurance plans to see what you might pay out of pocket. Here are some examples:

1. **GoodRx Calculator**
    - **How it works:** Enter the name of your medication, dosage, and amount you need. GoodRx shows prices at different pharmacies near you and gives you discount coupons.
    - **Example:** If you need Lipitor (atorvastatin) 20mg, enter this info into GoodRx. It might show that prices range from $10 to $30 and provide a coupon to lower the cost to $15.
    - **Available at:** www.goodrx.com
2. **SingleCare Calculator**
    - **How it works:** Like GoodRx, you put in your medication details, and SingleCare shows prices at local pharmacies and offers coupons.

- **Example:** Entering Metformin 500mg into SingleCare could show prices from $4 to $12, and you can get a coupon to pay as low as $5.
- **Available at:** www.singlecare.com

3. **Medicare Plan Finder**
   - **How it works:** This tool helps Medicare users compare Part D plans based on their medications and pharmacy choices. You enter your medication list, and it shows the estimated yearly cost for different plans.
   - **Example:** If you take medications like Lisinopril, Metformin, and Simvastatin, the Medicare Plan Finder shows the total estimated cost for each plan to help you pick the best one.
   - **Available at:** www.medicare.gov/plan-compare

4. **NeedyMeds Drug Discount Card Calculator**
   - **How it works:** NeedyMeds offers a card that lowers medication costs at pharmacies. Their calculator shows the discount for specific drugs.
   - **Example:** For Albuterol inhalers, the calculator might show a discount that reduces the price from $60 to $30 with the NeedyMeds card.
   - **Available at:** www.needymeds.org/drug-discount-card

5. **AARP Prescription Drug Calculator**
   - **How it works:** AARP has a tool for members to estimate prescription costs and find savings. Enter your medication details to see price comparisons and savings options.
   - **Example:** Entering Synthroid (levothyroxine) might show savings options that lower the cost from $25 to $10 per refill.
   - **Available at:** www.aarp.org

These online calculators help you understand medication pricing and insurance coverage. By using them, you can find the best prices and save money on your healthcare costs.

Wrapping it all up…

By using these tools and resources, you can take a proactive approach to managing your healthcare costs and ensuring you receive the best possible care. Keep these worksheets and templates handy, and don't hesitate to revisit them as your healthcare needs change. Remember, you have the power to make informed decisions, access free or low-cost vaccines, and take control of your healthcare journey.

CHAPTER 8: FINANCIAL ASSISTANCE FOR MEDICATIONS

Managing the high costs of medications can be tough, but there are many options available to help you. This chapter explores non-profit organizations, crowdfunding platforms, and government grants that can provide the support you need to afford your medications.

8.1 INTRODUCTION TO FINANCIAL ASSISTANCE

Financial assistance programs are here to help you manage the costs of necessary medications. Knowing about these resources and using them can make a big difference in your healthcare expenses. In this chapter, you'll find a comprehensive overview of non-profit organizations, crowdfunding platforms, and government grants that can provide the support you need.

8.2 NON-PROFIT ORGANIZATIONS

Several non-profit organizations offer financial assistance for medications. They provide grants, free medications, and other resources to those in need.

List and Description of Non-Profits

Patient Access Network (PAN) Foundation

- **Mission:** Helps underinsured patients with out-of-pocket costs for life-saving medications.

- **Benefits:** Offers grants to help cover co-pays, deductibles, and other expenses related to prescription medications.

- **Eligibility:** Based on financial need and diagnosis. Visit the PAN Foundation website to apply.

HealthWell Foundation

- **Mission:** Helps patients with chronic and life-altering illnesses afford their medical treatments.

- **Benefits:** Provides financial assistance for prescription co-payments, insurance premiums, and other related costs.

- **Eligibility:** Income-based eligibility criteria. Applications are available on the HealthWell Foundation website.

The Assistance Fund
- **Mission:** Provides financial support to individuals with serious or chronic diseases.

- **Benefits:** Covers costs such as co-pays, deductibles, and insurance premiums for approved medications and treatments.

- **Eligibility:** Financial need and specific disease criteria. Visit The Assistance Fund website for more details.

How to Apply for Help

1. **Identify Eligible Programs:** Research and find non-profits that support your specific condition or medication needs.

2. **Gather Required Documents:** Prepare necessary paperwork, like proof of income, insurance information, and medical prescriptions.

3. **Submit Applications:** Follow the application process on the organization's website. Many applications can be completed online.

Additional Tips:
- **Follow Up:** After submitting your application, follow up with the organization to check the status. Persistence can often help speed up the process.

- **Seek Help:** Many organizations have support lines or case managers who can assist you in filling out applications and gathering necessary documents.

8.3: CROWDFUNDING FOR MEDICAL EXPENSES

Crowdfunding is a popular way to raise funds for medical expenses, including medication costs. Platforms like GoFundMe allow you to create fundraising campaigns and receive donations from friends, family, and the community.

How to Use Crowdfunding Platforms

GoFundMe
- **Features:** Create personalized fundraising campaigns with details of your medical needs. Share your campaign on social media to reach more people.

- **Benefits:** Easy to set up and manage. No platform fee, but transaction fees apply to donations.

- **Tips for Success:** Be clear about your needs, update donors regularly, and thank them for their support.

YouCaring (Now part of GoFundMe)
- **Features:** Focuses on compassionate crowdfunding for personal and medical expenses. Offers tools for campaign promotion and donor management.

- **Benefits:** No platform fees, making it a cost-effective option for fundraising.

- **Tips for Success:** Share your story authentically, provide regular updates, and engage with your supporters.

Hack: When creating a crowdfunding campaign, include a compelling story with personal photos and updates. This helps potential donors connect with your cause and increases the likelihood of receiving donations.

Example:
John's Campaign: John needed $10,000 for his cancer treatment. He shared his story on GoFundMe, explaining his journey and how donations would help him. By sharing regular

updates and thanking donors, he raised the full amount in three months.

8.4: GOVERNMENT GRANTS AND PROGRAMS

Government grants and programs can provide substantial financial assistance for medication expenses. People with low incomes, seniors, and those with chronic conditions are often the ones these programs are aimed at.

Overview of Government Grants

Medicare Extra Help
- **Description:** A federal program that helps Medicare beneficiaries who don't have a lot of money or other means pay for their prescription drugs.

- **Benefits:** Covers premiums, deductibles, and co-pays for Medicare Part D prescription drug plans.

- **Eligibility:** Based on income and resources. Apply through the Social Security Administration website.

State Pharmaceutical Assistance Programs (SPAPs)

- **Description:** State-funded programs that provide financial assistance for prescription medications to eligible residents.

- **Benefits:** Varies by state but may include coverage for co-pays, deductibles, and medications not covered by Medicare Part D.

- **Eligibility:** Based on income, age, and residency. Check your state's health department website for specific details and application procedures.

How to Apply for Government Assistance

1. **Research Available Programs:** Visit official government websites or contact local health departments to learn about available grants and programs.

2. **Prepare Documentation:** Gather necessary documents, such as proof of income, medical prescriptions, and insurance information.

3. **Submit Applications:** Follow the application guidelines provided by the respective programs. Many applications can be completed online or through local assistance offices.

Additional Tips:
- **Keep Copies:** Always keep copies of your application and any correspondence. This can help if there are any issues or if you need to reapply.

- **Seek Local Help:** Many communities have local organizations or social workers who can help you navigate these programs and complete applications.

Wrapping it all up…

By using these financial assistance resources, you can significantly reduce your medication costs and ease the financial burden of managing your health. These programs are designed to support you, so don't hesitate to explore and apply for the help you need. Remember, you have the right to seek help and ensure you get the necessary medications without overwhelming costs.

FURTHER READING AND RESOURCES

To deepen your understanding of medication savings and healthcare cost management, here are some recommended websites and resources. These sources have been referenced throughout this book and provide additional valuable information.

Health Insurance and Medication Cost Topics

Centers for Medicare & Medicaid Services (CMS)
For a foundational understanding of health insurance basics and insights into primary vs. secondary insurance, visit the Centers for Medicare & Medicaid Services.
Available at: www.cms.gov

Kaiser Family Foundation (KFF)
Explore detailed explanations of health insurance topics, including prior authorization, formularies, and the appeals process at the Kaiser Family Foundation, a leader in health policy analysis.
Available at: www.kff.org

HealthCare.gov

For comprehensive guidance on navigating insurance formularies and cost savings, along with understanding your rights under insurance plans, check out HealthCare.gov.

Available at: www.healthcare.gov

National Association of InsuranceCommissioners (NAIC)

Gain insight into the appeals process and patient rights in health insurance from the National Association of Insurance Commissioners.

Available at: www.naic.org

Consumer Reports

For practical advice on dealing with medication refunds and rights, consider the resources available at Consumer Reports.

Available at: www.consumerreports.org

U.S. Food and Drug Administration (FDA)

For information on the differences between generic and brand-name drugs and how generics are approved, visit the FDA.

Available at: www.fda.gov

GoodRx

To find the best pharmacy deals and compare medication prices, GoodRx offers up-to-date pricing and discount information.

Available at: www.goodrx.com

NeedyMeds
Explore NeedyMeds for a wide range of information on discounts, coupons, and pharmaceutical assistance programs that can help reduce medication costs.
Available at: www.needymeds.org

Consumer Reports
For insights into alternative medications and strategies to save on prescription drugs, Consumer Reports provides valuable advice.
Available at: www.consumerreports.org

Medicare.gov
Specifically for Medicare-related information, including coverage details and updates, Medicare.gov is the official U.S. government site for Medicare. Available at: www.medicare.gov

Health Resources and Services Administration (HRSA)
For comprehensive details on the 340B Drug Pricing Program, which allows access to reduced-price medication in healthcare facilities, check out the HRSA site.
Available at: www.hrsa.gov

National Council on Aging (NCOA)
To learn more about State Pharmaceutical Assistance Programs and other support available for seniors, visit the National Council on Aging.
Available at: www.ncoa.org

Additional Sources for Financial Assistance and Government Programs

Medicaid.gov
Provides detailed information on Medicaid eligibility, benefits, and how to apply for coverage.
Available at:
www.medicaid.gov/medicaid/eligibility/index.html

InsureKidsNow.gov
An overview of the Children's Health Insurance Program (CHIP), its benefits, and enrollment process.
Available at: www.insurekidsnow.gov

VA.gov
Detailed information on eligibility, benefits, and how to enroll in the VA healthcare system.
Available at: www.va.gov/health-care/

Medicare Interactive
Information on State Pharmaceutical Assistance Programs (SPAPs), eligibility criteria, and how to apply.
Available at: www.medicareinteractive.org/get-answers/

PAN Foundation
Provides financial assistance to underinsured patients for out-of-pocket costs associated with life-saving medications.
Available at: www.panfoundation.org

HealthWell Foundation
Helps patients with chronic and life-altering illnesses afford their medical treatments.
Available at: www.healthwellfoundation.org

The Assistance Fund
Provides financial support to individuals with serious or chronic diseases.
Available at: **www.tafcares.org**

Free Vaccine Resources

Vaccines for Children (VFC) Program
Information about the VFC program and locating nearby VFC providers.
Available at: www.cdc.gov

National Association of County and City Health Officials (NACCHO)
Find local health departments that offer free or low-cost vaccinations.
Available at: www.naccho.org

Health Resources and Services Administration (HRSA)

Locate Federally Qualified Health Centers (FQHCs) for free or reduced-cost vaccinations. Available at: <u>findahealthcenter.hrsa.gov</u>

These resources will provide further insights and support as you continue your journey to manage and reduce your healthcare and medication costs. By staying informed and proactive, you can make the most of the available tools and strategies to achieve better health and financial stability.

CONCLUSION

You made it to the end—and I'm really glad you stuck with it.

This book was written to give you real, usable tools to help you save on medication and understand the parts of the system that usually feel like a mess. Not everything here will apply to everyone—but if even one chapter gave you some clarity or saved you money, then it's already done what I hoped it would.

Here's a quick look back at what we covered:

Key Takeaways

Understanding Health Insurance

- You've got the basics down—terms like deductibles, co-pays, and coinsurance.

- You know how primary and secondary insurance can work together, and why that matters.

Navigating Insurance for Medications

- You understand what prior authorizations are and how to handle them.

- You've learned how to check your plan's formulary to find more affordable medication options.

Finding Ways to Cut Costs

- You know when to ask for generics and how to compare prices across pharmacies.
- You've seen how mail-order options and patient assistance programs can lower your out-of-pocket costs.
- You're aware of how to look for therapeutic alternatives if your current medication is too expensive.

Using Discounts and Savings Programs

- You've got a list of places to find discounts—like cards, manufacturer savings, and coupons.
- You know how to bring cost concerns to your doctor without feeling awkward or uncomfortable.

Knowing Your Rights

- You've learned how to appeal insurance denials, ask about refunds, and push back when something doesn't feel fair.
- You know where to start if you ever need legal or advocacy support.

Government Support Options

- You've walked through the basics of Medicare, Medicaid, VA Health Care, and CHIP.
- You've learned how programs like SPAPs and 340B can open up more affordable access to medications.

Financial Help for Medications

- You've got a list of trusted non-profits, grant programs, and crowdfunding ideas to lean on if money is tight.
- You've seen how places like the PAN Foundation and HealthWell Foundation can step in when insurance doesn't.

What You Can Keep Doing

Stay Curious

- Keep checking in on your coverage and pricing—it can change more often than you'd expect.
- Keep asking your doctor or pharmacist if there's a more affordable option that still works.

Stay Organized

- Write down your current medications, insurance benefits, and any costs you're tracking.
- Use the checklists and tools from this book if they help simplify things.

Stay Connected

- Be honest with your providers about what's affordable for you. It's not complaining—it's advocating.
- Make sure your full medication list is shared with every provider you see.

Use What Works

- Try apps, reminder tools, or telehealth when it fits. Small tools can make a big difference when your brain's juggling a million other things.

Final Thoughts

This isn't about doing everything perfectly. It's about making small, smart choices that add up—and knowing where to turn when things don't go as planned.

If this book helped, I'd love it if you'd leave a review. It helps other folks find the same kind of support—and it helps me keep writing more resources like this one.

If you want to go deeper, check out *"Your Pharmacist's Guide to Saving Money and Staying Healthy."* It brings together the bigger picture in one place.

But for now, just remember this:

You don't have to do it all alone. You've already started—and that counts.

Thanks for letting me be part of your healthcare journey. I hope what you found here helps you save more, stress less, and feel just a little more confident every time you pick up a prescription.

ACKNOWLEDGMENTS

Before we close this chapter, I just want to say thank you. This book didn't come together on its own, and so many people helped make it happen.

To the moms, patients, and caregivers who've shared your stories and questions with me over the years—you're the reason this book exists. Your honesty, your strength, and the way you keep showing up inspired every single page.

To my family and friends—especially my husband and daughters—you are everything. Thank you for cheering me on, keeping me grounded, and giving me the space to write. I couldn't have done this without you.

And finally—to you. Thank you for letting me walk beside you. Writing this felt like chatting with a friend, and I hope it brought you a little more confidence, a little more calm, and maybe even a few smiles when you needed them most.

Here's to the love you give, the strength you show, and the quiet, powerful ways you keep supporting yourself and your loved ones.

Rhowela A. Friel, PharmD

ABOUT THE AUTHOR

Hi—I'm Rhowela Albana Friel. I'm a pharmacist, a mom of two girls, a wife, and someone who's spent years helping families make sense of healthcare.

Pharmacy has always been part of my story. My mom was a pharmacist, my dad a family doctor, and I grew up in the Philippines watching them care for people through our little family-owned pharmacy. Some of my earliest memories are of sitting behind the counter, watching people come in with questions and leave with real help. That's what healthcare has always meant to me: showing up when it matters most.

After moving to the U.S. at 13, I kept following that path. I started working at CVS after high school, became a pharmacist, and grew into roles that let me support both patients and pharmacy teams—as a Pharmacy Manager, a Supervisor, and later a District Manager for specialty pharmacies serving underserved communities. These days, I'm a

Clinical Pharmacist working with state programs to improve access to essential medications.

But nothing has shaped me more than becoming a mom. My girls have taught me more than any textbook ever could. They're the reason I started writing—because I know how hard it can be to figure things out while still being the one everyone counts on.

This book came from that place. From wanting to offer something real and helpful. From knowing what it's like to be tired, unsure, and still trying your best.

I don't have all the answers—but I'll keep showing up with what I do know, and what I've learned through both my career and this messy, beautiful, everyday life.

There's more ahead—more books, more support, and more real talk for real life. I'm so glad you're here.

MORE SUPPORT

Thank you again for picking up this book. I hope it brought you a little more clarity, a little less stress, and maybe even a few deep breaths when you needed them most.

If you're wondering what comes next—I've got you.

You can find me at rhowelaafriel.com, where I've gathered everything I've created (and am still creating) to help you feel steady, supported, and prepared—without the overwhelm.

Here's what you'll find there:
- **Books** – A look at what I've already written and what's coming next. Each one is built to walk alongside you.
- **The Blog** – Stories, tips, and encouragement—some personal, some practical—all written like we're chatting over coffee.
- **Recommended Products** – A no-stress roundup of the things I actually use and love, all in one place.
- **The Shop** – Simple tools like checklists, guides, and downloads to make the everyday feel a little easier.
- **Contact** – Have a question or just want to connect? I'd love to hear from you.

The site's easy to explore—so stop by anytime. I'll be there, building more resources to help you take care of yourself and the people you love.

INDEX

340B Drug Pricing Program 59, 87
Affordable Alternatives 36
Alternative Medications 35
Appeal Process 40, 67
Assistance Programs .. 37, 57, 66, 83, 88
Building Your Case 41
Case Study.30, 36, 44, 62, 63, 64
Checklist 37, 47, 66, 69
Children's Health Insurance Program 54, 88
CHIP 49, 54, 55, 88, 92
COB 14
Co-insurance 12
Coordination of Benefits .. 14
Co-pay 12
coupons 9, 18, 27, 33, 34, 37, 64, 65, 66, 73, 87, 92
Crowdfunding 80
Deductible 12
Discount Programs 34, 37, 63
discounts 9, 33, 34, 38, 61, 87, 92
Dosage Adjustments 36
Dual Eligibles 53
Filing an Appeal 41
Financial assistance programs 77
Formularies 12, 19, 21
Getting a Refund 42, 43
Government grants 82
Hack 12, 14, 18, 21, 26, 28, 34, 36, 40, 43, 51, 52, 54, 55, 56, 58, 60, 61, 81

Health Insurance Basics 11
Health Resources and Services Administration 59, 61, 87, 90
How to Choose a Health Insurance Plan 15
How to Request a Prior 19
HRSA 59, 60, 61, 87, 90
Legal Help and Advocacy .45
Manufacturer Coupons 34, 64
Maximizing Savings 33, 37
Medicaid 51, 52, 53, 54, 55, 57, 58, 59, 71, 85, 88, 92
Medicare 30, 49, 50, 51, 53, 54, 57, 58, 59, 62, 63, 74, 82, 83, 85, 87, 88, 92
Medicare Part A 50
Medicare Part B 50
Medicare Part C 50
Medicare Part D ... 50, 53, 54, 57, 58, 59, 62, 63, 82, 83
medication refunds 39, 42, 86
Medication Tiers 20
Multiple Policies 14
non-profit organizations .. 37, 77, 78
PAPs 29, 64, 66
Patient Assistance Programs 29, 64
Patients' Legal Rights 45
Paying Without Insurance .28
Pill Splitting 37
Practical Example 13
Price Comparison Tools ... 27
Price Gap Explained 26
Primary Insurance 13

Pro Tip 18
recommended websites 85
Refund from the Pharmacy
   42
resources 64, 82, 85
Right to Choose Providers 45
Right to Information 45
Right to Privacy 45
Secondary Insurance ... 13, 14

Therapeutic Alternatives . 31, 32
Therapeutic Substitution .. 36
Tier 1 .... 20, 21
Tier 2 20
Tier 3 20
Tier 4 20
VA Health Care 55, 92

www.ingramcontent.com/pod-product-compliance
Lightning Source LLC
Chambersburg PA
CBHW050115230526
45470CB00004B/1838